The ups and downs of a boy and his dog

Close observation of the scene top left will reveal two of the strip's main characters – Wellington, a member of the human race, and Boot, a member of the canine race – shown here about to indulge in a ping-pong of claim and counter-claim as to the rightful ownership of a sausage sarnie.

The boy, Wellington, as a junior member of Homo Sapiens, the Senior Service of the Animal Kingdom, believes the captive bangers to be his by right – and anyway he designed and constructed the sandwich.

The dog, Boot, will have no truck with such slipshod thinking. After all, he reasons, the pup hasn't even yet learned to walk on all fours – and if God had meant him to make his own sandwiches he wouldn't have invented Wellington.

Moreover Boot believes himself to be no mere mutt, but an eighteenth century nobleman. He puts his present predicament down to the curse of a gipsy wench with whom he'd become embroiled. When he unwisely tried to become unembroiled, he woke up several centuries later wearing a loosely fitting fur coat he can't recall having ordered from the tailors.

Time after time he has tried to explain the situation to Wellington, but the lad, in spite of showing some glimmerings of intelligence, just doesn't comprehend. Another reason why Boot's convinced that Darwin muffed it. The evolutionary ladder leads down, not up.

However in spite of their differences they remain constant friends, as depicted in the right hand corner – showing Wellington having just won Boot's undying love and affection by announcing they'd won the Pools.
He was lying, of course.

The downs and downs of a boy and a girl (loosely speaking)

Here we see Maisie and Marlon engaged in conversation. Or, to be absolutely correct, Maisie engaged in conversation with Marlon's feet. Not that Maisie habitually talks to feet but they happen to be the location of Marlon's brain; which he keeps in his boots to prevent it wandering off and doing a bit of freelance thinking.

Anyway in Marlon's case it doesn't much matter which end is addressed, the end result's the same. The flickering light of comprehension appears in his eyes – but it says 'Tilt'!

Nonetheless Maisie nurtures an overwhelming passion for the witless wonder and pursues him with zeal, and ropes, and nets, and traps – in fact with anything she thinks will captivate him while at the same time restraining his violent struggles.

Marlon does not return Maisie's affections – an activity you can see him working hard at lower on the page. Why can this be? After all she's as attractive as a sackful of old Army Boots, and has a great deal of talent – as a pest exterminator. One shriek from Maisie has pests frantically vacating the woodwork within a two-mile radius.

In spite of these attractions Marlon avoids Maisie's embrace because he knows kissing weakens a man. It did for his uncle who used to drink two bottles of rum a day, to overcome his shyness, and then ran about chasing women. As Marlon says – who wants to wear themselves out at ninety-eight through chasing women?

The even further downs of a mis-spent childhood.

Maisie's life is not a bed of roses, and she walks not a petal-strewn path. Her bed is more likely to be filled with frogs, and her path strewn with tintacks – both aids to gracious living donated by her little brother, Baby Grumpling, who was in turn donated by her mother; an event which caused Maisie to regard her mother as having a somewhat warped sense of humour – since Maisie had been expecting a puppy.

Baby Grumpling is credited with such inventions as the worm sandwich, the Polyfilla blancmange, the original spider-in-the-bath (which he later diversified into the spider-in-everything), the AAAAAGH! cushion (a version of the whoopie cushion – but stuffed with hedgehogs) and other devices to accelerate mankind's descent down the slippery slope. Oh, yes – he invented that too.

Maisie's mother goes out to work and father's a long-distance lorry driver (he was a short-distance driver until Baby Grumpling's arrival) so Maisie is frequently left minding her little brother, who needs a minder the way King Kong needs a bodyguard. Maisie's subsequent lifestyle makes for erratic behaviour and violent mood-changes.

Contrast the scene on the left, showing her praying for merciful release, with the one below, where she's depicted in execution of a more desperate ploy. While Baby Grumpling's occupied with thoughts of a goldfish sandwich she plans a savage attack from behind, subsequently throwing suspicion on the fish.

I THOUGHT FLIES WERE SPOSED TO GO TO SLEEP IN THE WINTER

THEY ARE

BUT THEY CAN'T COUNT ON ME BEING HERE WHEN THEY WAKE UP

SO I'VE GOT A WIDEAWAKE FOLLOWING OF EXTREMELY ANXIOUS FLIES

T258

HEY YOU TWO

DID YOU KNOW DIRTY McSQUIRTY'S GOT ANXIOUS FLIES?

I CAN'T ABIDE SMUTTY STORIES

T259

Maurice Dodd

T260

AH - DIRTY McSQUIRTY

I THOUGHT I'D FIND YOU HERE

D'YOU REALLY BELIEVE THESE FLIES ARE IN AN ANXIETY STATE?

OH YES

T261

HOW CAN YOU TELL?

OH - THE USUAL INDICATIONS

WORRIED EXPRESSION, HOLLOW CHEEKS, THE OCCASIONAL TREMOR....

T288

T289

U40 Maurice Dodd

Panel 1: I CAN'T HAVE YOU IN THE HOUSE ALL DAY UNDER MY FEET, I'VE GOT TO GET YOU OUT INTO THE FRESH AIR, BABY GRUMPLING

I KNOW IT'S VERY COLD SO I'LL BUNDLE YOU UP NICE AND WARM

Panel 2: OUT YOU GO THEN—HAVE A NICE PLAY

Panel 3: play? i can't even **move**

U41

Panel 1: NOW RUN ABOUT AND GET SOME EXERCISE, BABY GRUMPLING

TRY OUT YOUR LOVELY NEW MOON-BOOTS

Panel 2: it's very traumatic for a child to detect deception in an adult

most especially when it concerns ones **own** mother

Panel 3: apart from the obvious inference with regard to my own intelligence

one hardly appreciates being placed on the level of a cretin

Panel 4: **moon-boots indeed**

it takes her half a day to do five-minutes shopping in the **high street**

Maurice Dodd

WELL NOW—
THIS GREAT KETCHUP
CAPER YOU ARE
DESCRIBING...

U56

WERE
KETCHUP THE ONLY
COMESTIBLE INVOLVED
—NO VEGETABLES?

NO—
WHY?

(SIGH) I
WERE RATHER HOPING
FOR NEWS OF A
CABINET LEEK

LISTEN, B.H.
THIS STORY IS ABOUT A
BUNCH OF **CHILDREN** SQUIRTING
KETCHUP AT EACH OTHER
AND **THAT'S ALL**

U57

—NO DRUGS,
NO BOOZE, NO SEX, NO
CABINET LEAKS, NO SHOCKING
DISCLOSURES, NO ESPIONAGE,
NO....

YOU'RE NEVER
GOING TO TELL ME NOT
EVEN **ONE** OF THEM USED
A **NAUGHTY WORD**

U68

U69

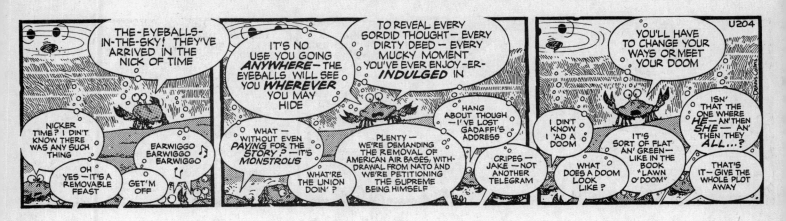
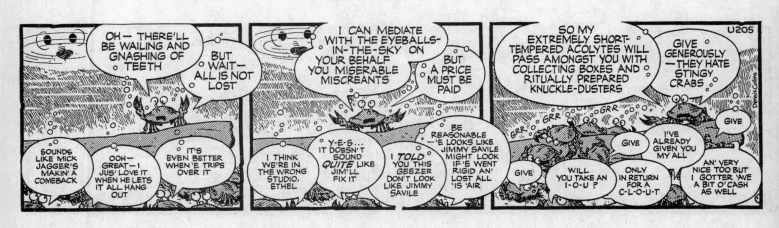

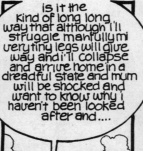

DON'T MISS
PEACE AT CHRISTMAS? THERE ARE STILL SIX DAYS TO GO!
THE WORLD OF ANDY CAPP
Bumper Issue
ON THE SIXTH DAY OF CHRISTMAS-!!
Cartoons by
Reg Smythe
AVAILABLE FROM YOUR NEWSAGENT NOW!